Micro Rambler Series

Shotley Peninsula Walks

15 Linked Circular Walks on the Shotley Peninsula

Geoff Gostling

ISBN 0-9525478-1-3

Printed by Portman Press
Published by G.J.Gostling
Copyright © G.J.Gostling

Cover Picture: Freston Tower

To the best of my knowledge, the information supplied in this book is accurate, and rights of way were correct at the time of writing. No responsibility is accepted for acts of trespass, problems arising from rerouting or closing of paths, or misread instructions.

CONTENTS

	Introduction		3
	Places		4

Walks

1	Brantham	(5m, 8½km)	6
2	Stutton, Holbrook Bay	(4½m, 7½km)	8
3	Stutton, Alton Water	(6m, 9½km)	10
4	Lower Holbrook, Harkstead	(5m, 8km)	12
5	Harkstead Circular	(3½m, 5½km)	14
6	Harkstead, Ewarton	(5½m, 8½km)	16
7	Shotley Point, Ewarton	(5m, 8km)	18
8	Shotley, Marina, Shotley Church	(5m, 8km)	20
9	Shotley Church circular	(4m, 6½km)	22
10	Pin Mill, Clamp House, NT Woods	(2½m, 4km)	24
11	Pin Mill, Cat House, Woolverstone	(3m, 4½km)	26
12	Freston, Woolverstone Church	(4½m, 7½km)	28
13	Holbrook, Freston	(5m, 8km)	30
14	Holbrook, Alton Water	(6m, 9½km)	32
15	Alton Water Circular	(8m, 12km)	34
	Outline Map of Shotley Peninsula		36

INTRODUCTION

All walks in this book are in the area bounded by Wherstead, Brantham and Shotley, known as the Shotley Peninsula. It's one of the unspoilt parts of Suffolk.

If you complete them all, you'll not only have explored most of the shoreline, but will also have walked a large part of the 'internal' footpaths. There are some you'll have walked twice, but always in a different direction.

The average length is 7½km (nearly 5m), but because most are linked together, sharing a side with one on an adjoining page, you can join 2 or more together to make longer walks.

For each walk, there's a sketch map on the left hand page, with instructions on the right. When opened, the book fits a standard map case, or A4 plastic sleeve. When closed it's of a size to fit most pockets.

All walks use rights of way, and, where necessary, unclassified roads. Some small use is made of classified roads to get from one path to another. Whatever the type of road, please take due care.

How to Get There The main access routes are shown on the outline map on page 36. Circled numbers show the approximate start points of each walk.

Rights of Way. 'Right of Way' means that you have a right of passage, but no right to stray from the path. You also have a right to expect that paths be unobstructed. Clearly farm land has to be ploughed at times, but farmers should reinstate paths within 2 weeks if weather permits.

Signed Paths: You'll find frequent use of the term 'signed path' in this book. Unfortunately there's a tendency for footpath signs to disappear in this area. Between the time of writing and the time of publication, some of those referred to may have disappeared, whilst some not referred to will be in place. Please bear this possibility in mind when following the instructions.

Directions: These are meant to be self-contained, and a sketch-map is provided opposite each text. However, you may find O.S. Landranger Sheet 169 useful in getting to start points. Grid references are given for the start of each walk.

Map Scale. The scale of the maps is about 4cm to 1km (2½" to the mile). The outline map on page 36 is about 2cm to 1km.

Distances: These are given in metres/kilometres. If you're more comfortable with yards and miles, just remember that, roughly, 1 metre is 1 yard, 400m is a quarter of a mile, 1½km is a mile and 8km is 5 miles.

Times: These will depend on your speed and whether you want to stop and look at views, wildlife etc. Remember that 2km on a river wall will take considerably longer than 2km on a metalled lane.

Transport. Bus routes are provided and are believed correct at time of writing, but you're advised to obtain an Eastern Counties timetable before planning walks based on bus connections.

Footwear. River walls are often overgrown and can be rough going. Paths and tracks may be muddy. Good stout shoes or boots are advisable.

Tides: Walk 5 is along the beach for some distance, and you shouldn't attempt this anywhere near high tide. Walk 9 includes 150m on the marsh. Please be aware of tides before setting out on these.

Cliff Subsidence Yes, there are cliffs round the peninsula, although they're not very high. Cliff subsidence is a frequent occurrence. Whether walking on the cliffs or below, please be aware of the dangers, unless you want to become a permanent part of the landscape.

Country Code. Help care for the countryside, by observing a few simple rules:

> Guard against risk of fire;
> Fasten gates;
> Keep pets under control;
> Keep to public rights of way;
> Use gates and stiles to cross fences;
> Take all litter home;
> Leave livestock alone;
> Don't pollute water;
> Protect wildlife, plants and trees;
> Don't make unnecessary noise.

Places of Interest

Brantham: Selected in the late 1800's for the site of a Xylonite works (Now Storeys Industrial Products). The church contains a religious painting by John Constable. There are several pubs, but the closest one for Walk 1 is the Bull.

Stutton: A pleasant village. There are some charming cottages and a nice 14th century church in Lower Street. Two pubs, Gardener's Arms and Kings Head.

Alton Water: Reservoir for the Ipswich area. Alton Hall and Tattingstone Hall were flooded when this was created in 1976. There is a path/cycleway all the way round. There's also a Visitors centre, with a cafe, a cycle hire centre, and a sailing centre. There are 2 Pay and Display car parks.

Holbrook: Best known for the Royal Hospital School, once a boarding school for the sons of naval officers - this is no longer a pre-requisite, and it's now co-educational. All Saint's church has connections with Anne Boleyn. There are 2 pubs, The Compasses and The Swan.

Harkstead: A pleasant village, with a fine 14th century church. 1 pub, the Baker's Arms - Good home-cooked food is usually available.

Erwarton: (Sometimes spelt Arwarton) Small village with a fine Hall and an interesting Jacobean brick gatehouse. Anne Boleyn was related to early owners, and visited them with Henry VIII. Her heart was supposedly buried in a casket in Erwarton Church. 1 pub, the Queen's Head!

Shotley: Known to many boy entrants in the Royal Navy, this was the home of HMS Ganges; not a ship but a shore-based training camp. There's an interesting church away from the main part of the village. It lacks a tower, which fell down in 1638. Tower-less or not, it's well worth a visit. It's worth taking a look at the nearby naval cemetery as well. There's one pub in Shotley, the Rose, and one at Shotley Gate, The Bristol Arms.

Pin Mill: Location of one of the most photographed pubs in Suffolk, the Butt and Oyster. The name Pin Mill probably comes from a watermill on the River Pindle which joined the Orwell at this point.

Chelmondiston: Small village with a modern church, courtesy Adolf Hitler - one of his flying bombs destroyed the original in 1944. There are 2 pubs, The Forester's Arms and The Red Lion.

Woolverstone: A small village, known best for Woolverstone Hall, previously an ILEA boarding school, but now run by Ipswich High School for Girls. There's a 19th century church in Woolverstone Hall park. In the grounds of the marina is a private house known as Cat House, named because the owners used to warn smugglers by placing a cat in the window.

Freston: Famous for it's tower, which doesn't quite deserve to be called a folly. It's made up of 6 rooms, one above the other. It's not open to the public, which is a shame because the views must be spectacular. There's 1 pub, The Boot, a pleasant pub with a varied menu.

Tattingstone: When the valley was flooded in 1976 this became a lakeside village. A survivor of the flooding was the Tattingstone Wonder, a block of cottages built with the facade of a church, possibly by a landowner who felt his view was incomplete. There's only one pub on the route of one of these walks, and that's The Orange Box which shares premises with the Post Office. (See Walk 15).

....

I hope you'll enjoy walking on the Shotley peninsula. I've done my best to keep the book simple and accurate, but please take careful note of the text. Missing an instruction, for instance, could be disastrous, and send you hopelessly in the wrong direction. Check with the sketch map at frequent intervals to make sure the instructions make sense.

WALK 1

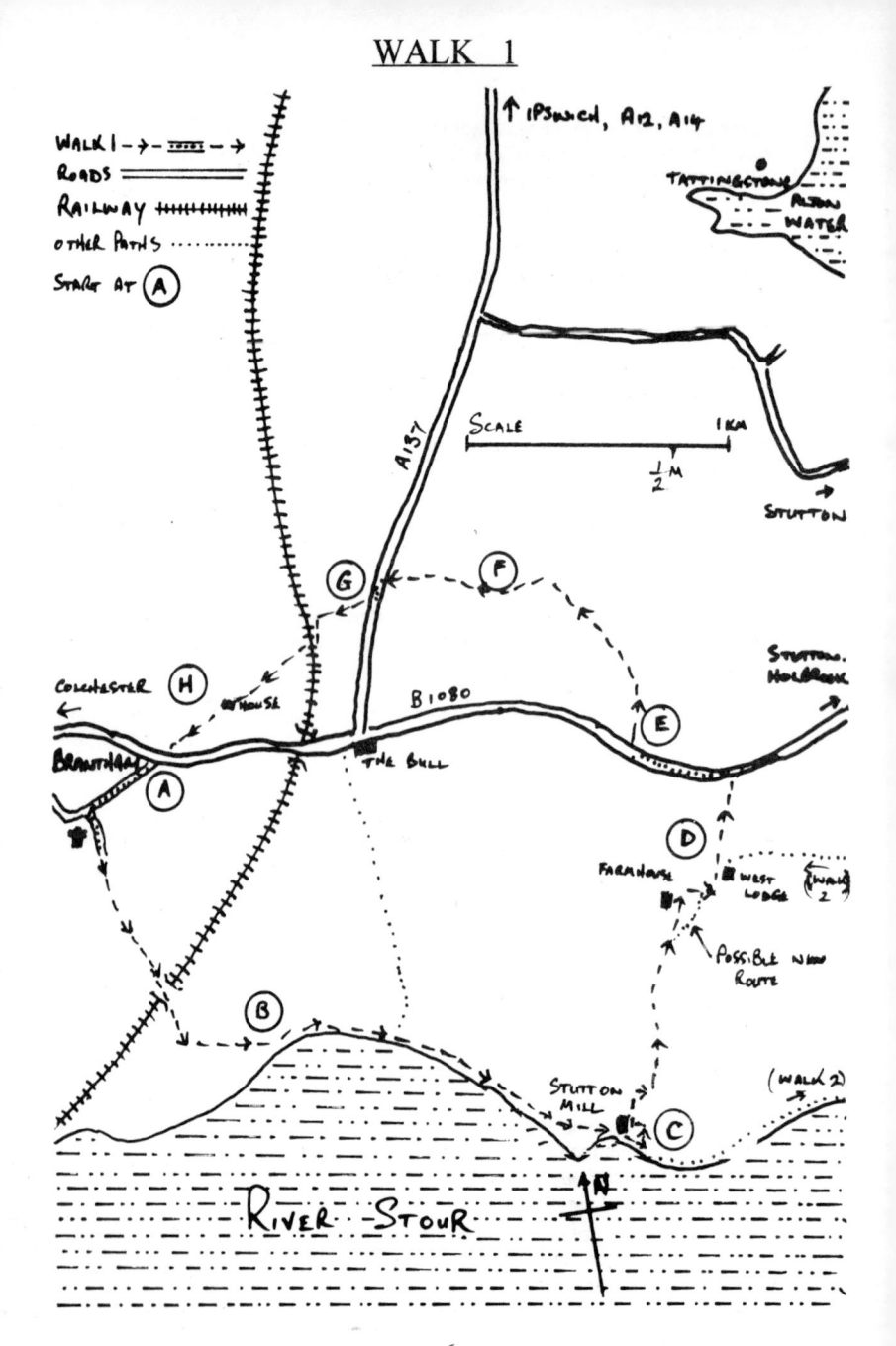

Walk 1

Distance: 8½km (5m) 2-2½ hours
Start Point: Church Lane, Brantham (GR 115345)
Route: Brantham Church, Stutton Shore, Stutton Mill
Pub: Brantham Bull (800m)
Bus Services: 96, 96A, 97a, 639
Car Parking: Lay-by near the Ipswich end of Church Lane**

There are two entrances to Church Lane from the main road. Use the lay-by near the top of the one nearest the Brantham Bull

A: Walk down Church Lane and go down the lane to the left of the church. Cross the bridge over the railway, and continue down towards the river. Shortly before the track turns right at the bottom of the hill, go half left down to a stile. Cross the stile, turn left and follow the track to the river wall in about 300m.

B: Climb onto the wall and continue in the same direction for about 1200m bringing you to the colourful Stutton Mill, now a private house.

C: Go straight past the house, to turn left on a permissive path at the end of the paddock, taking you along the edge of a wood, then down to the back of the house and out onto a lane. Stay on the lane for about 1½km, passing a cream coloured house. (Queech Farm - at the time of writing, a road is being built bypassing this, which may become the right-of-way - please take note of signs to this effect.) Soon after this, you'll pass a red-brick cottage called West Lodge.

D: Continue up the road past West Lodge to a main road in about 400m, and turn left. Stay on the road for about 400m, using the verge where possible

E: After crossing a bridge go through an opening on the right, then go through a gateway to continue on the other side of the hedge. Follow this track along between stream and hedge, soon entering a field. Continue along the field edge. At the end of the field go through the gate, turn sharp left with the field-edge then cross the field to walk along next to the stream.

F: In about 300m cross the stream over a concrete bridge, and continue along the right-hand side over a very marshy area to reach the road in about 300m. Turn left on the road (This is the main A137, so take care.)

G: After 100m on the road, cross a stile on the right onto a footpath along a field edge. Cross the railway in 300m, and continue up the field on the other side and into a copse. ***The right of way soon leaves the copse, and keeps left round the copse and house. However, local usage seems to be to stay on the main track to the right of the house and then to turn left***. On the far side of the house take a path across the field to the far corner. (If the path isn't clear, aim slightly left of some houses). This brings you out opposite Church Lane.

WALK 2

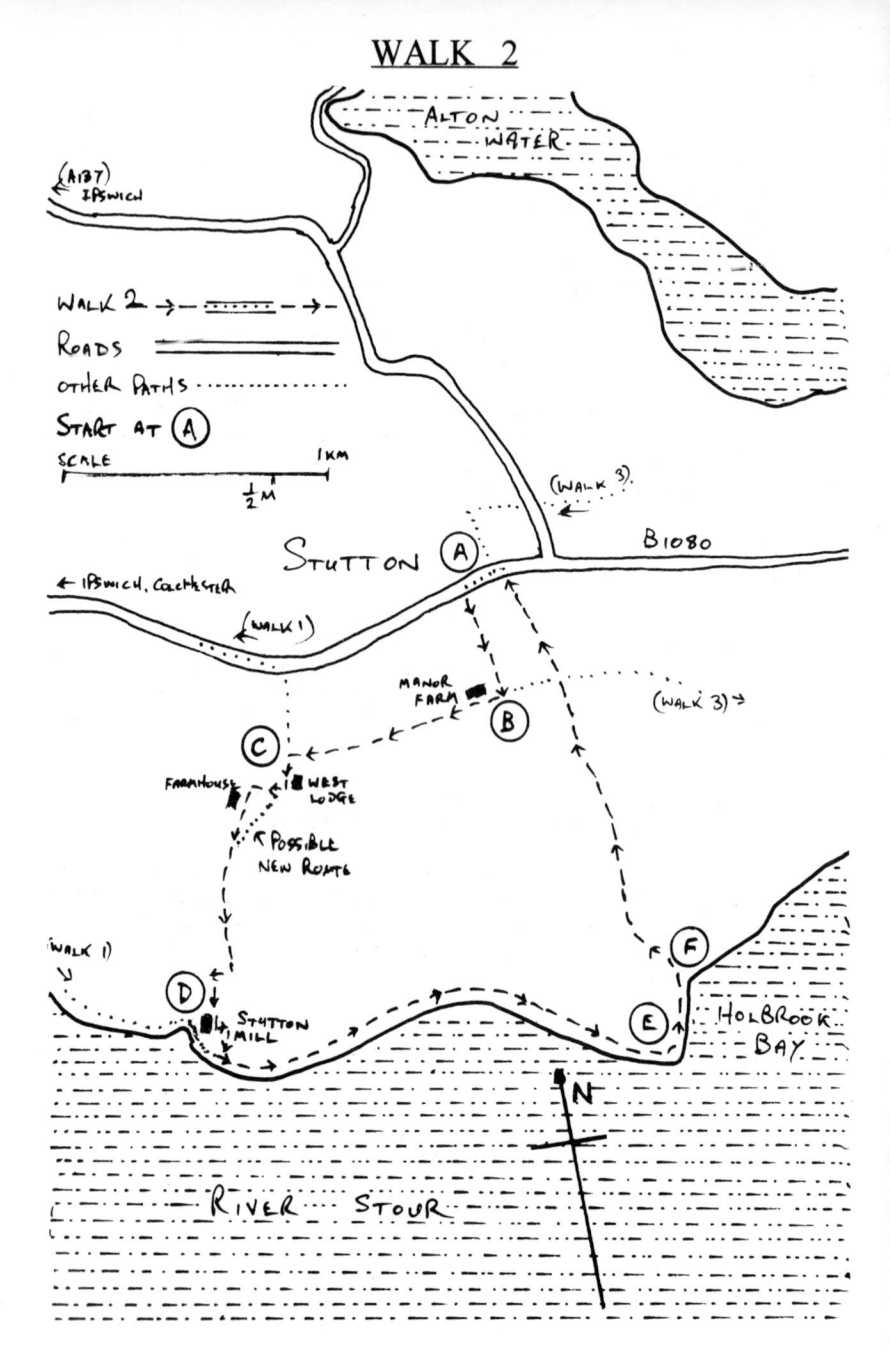

Walk 2

Distance: 7½km (4½m) 1½-2 hours
Start Point: Stutton Community Hall (GR 144347)
Route: Stutton Mill, Holbrook Bay, Stutton
Pub: Gardener's Arms (500m)
Bus Services: 96, 97a, 639
Car Parking: Concessionary parking on grass at Stutton Community Hall

A: Leave the car park, turn right, then in about 50m turn left down Manor Lane. Walk down to the T-junction.

B: Turn right at the T-junction, and stay on this track for about 1km to another T-junction, crossing the drive to Stutton Hall on the way.

C: Turn left at this second T-junction, passing a cottage called West Lodge, then shortly afterwards a cream-coloured farmhouse. (This is Queech Farm. Please note that, at the time of writing, a 'short cut' is being built bypassing the farm, and this may become the right of way - please observe any footpath signs to this effect) Continue on the lane down towards the river.

D: Just before entering the gate at Stutton Mill, take a signed permissive path to the left along the back of the building. Follow the signs taking you round a paddock, then turn left when you reach the river bank.

Follow this pleasant path along the river bank for about 2km. (25-35 minutes walk). The edges of the shallow cliffs along this path are crumbling away, so don't walk too close to the edge.

E: Eventually the river bank swings sharp left into Holbrook Bay, and the whole of the river as far as Felixstowe and Parkeston Quay comes into view.

F: About 300m after turning into Holbrook Bay, turn left onto a well-used track, lined with oak trees, taking you away from the river. Stay on this track all the way back to Stutton. When you reach the road, the Community Hall is about 100m to your left.

WALK 3

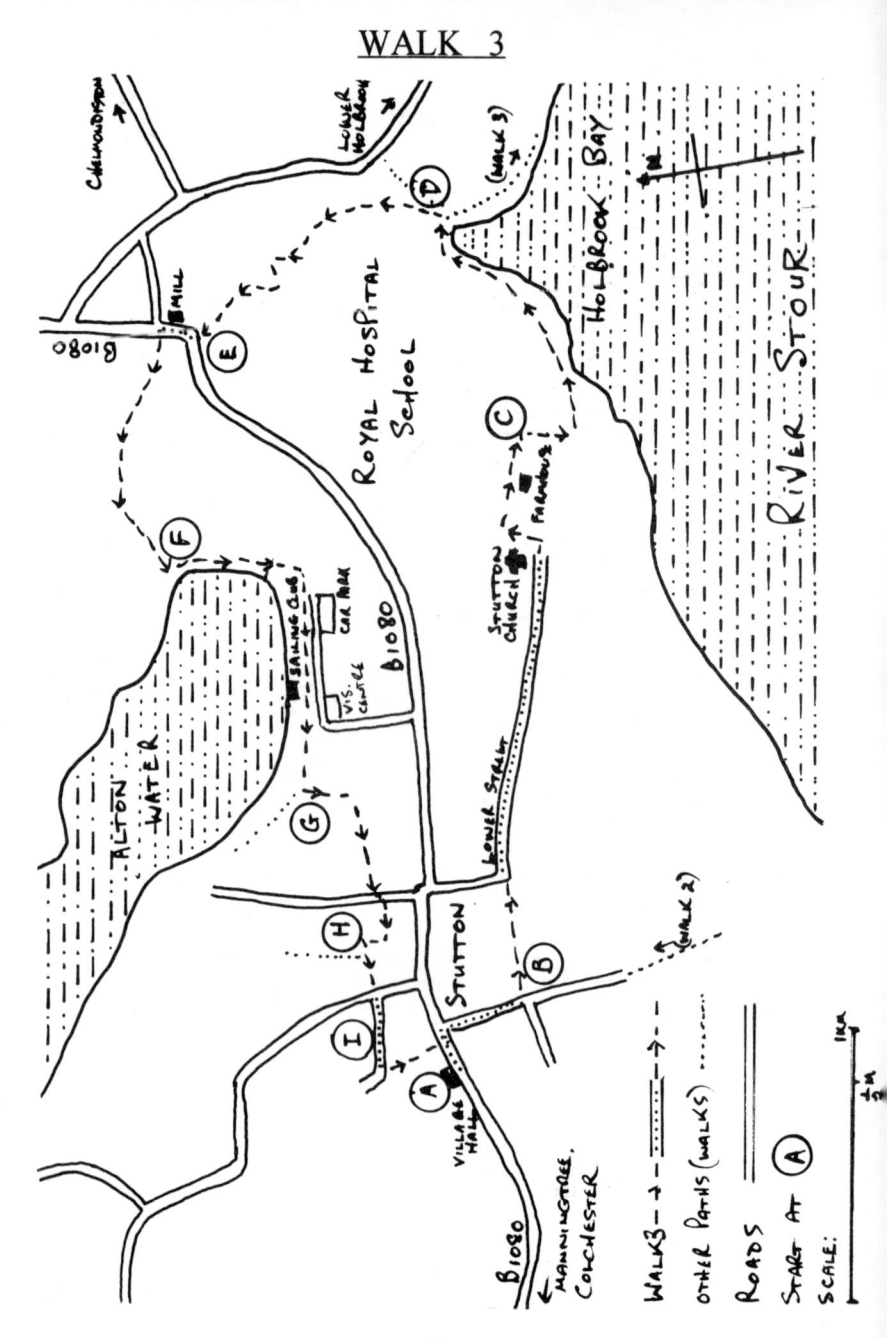

Walk 3

Distance: 9½km (6m) 2-2½ hours
Start Point: Stutton Community Hall (GR 144347)
Route: Stutton Church, Holbrook Bay, Alton Water
Pub: Gardener's Arms (400m)
Bus Services: 96, 97a, 639
Car Parking: Concessionary parking on grass at Stutton Community Hall.

A: Leave the car park, turn left and in about 100m turn right down a metalled lane.

B: After about 400m, turn left on a field-edge track (opposite a lane on the right). In about 400m you'll emerge on a narrow road (Lower Street). Go straight on here, and in about 1km, after passing the church, follow the footpath round to the left. Ignore the first gateway on the right, and about 50m after this turn right down the field aiming to the left of a farmhouse.

C: After the farmhouse, go straight on for about 100m, then turn right on a signed permissive path taking you to some steps up the river wall. Turn left on the wall and follow it to the boat shed in Holbrook Creek. Descend to the track below.

D: Follow the track past the boat shed, and about 50m after passing a gated entrance to a private wood, turn left on a well-trodden path along the left bank of a reedy stream. Stay on this path until you reach the road near Holbrook Mill, following the stream for all but the last 100m or so.

E: Turn right on the road, and after passing the mill turn left on a gated path through some poplars. Follow this track to pass a water treatment plant on your left, then continue uphill to reach Alton Water.

F: Turn left through the gate to walk along the bank of the reservoir. Follow the edge, passing a car park and sailing club. After passing the Visitors Centre up to your left, follow the cycle/footpath for another 300m to reach a stile on the left.

G: Cross the stile, and go through to the other side of the hedge. Follow the field edge with the hedge on your left all the way to a metalled lane. Turn left in the lane, and shortly afterwards, turn right on a narrow path next to a house. In about 100m the path swings right then left again round a cottage.

H: Stay on the main path, ignoring the footpath sign to your right, to bring you out on a narrow road in about 100m.

I: Go straight across the road into Woodfield Lane, and follow it for about 400m until it bends sharply to the right. At this point take an unsigned field path to the left, to bring you back to the road next to the village hall.

WALK 4

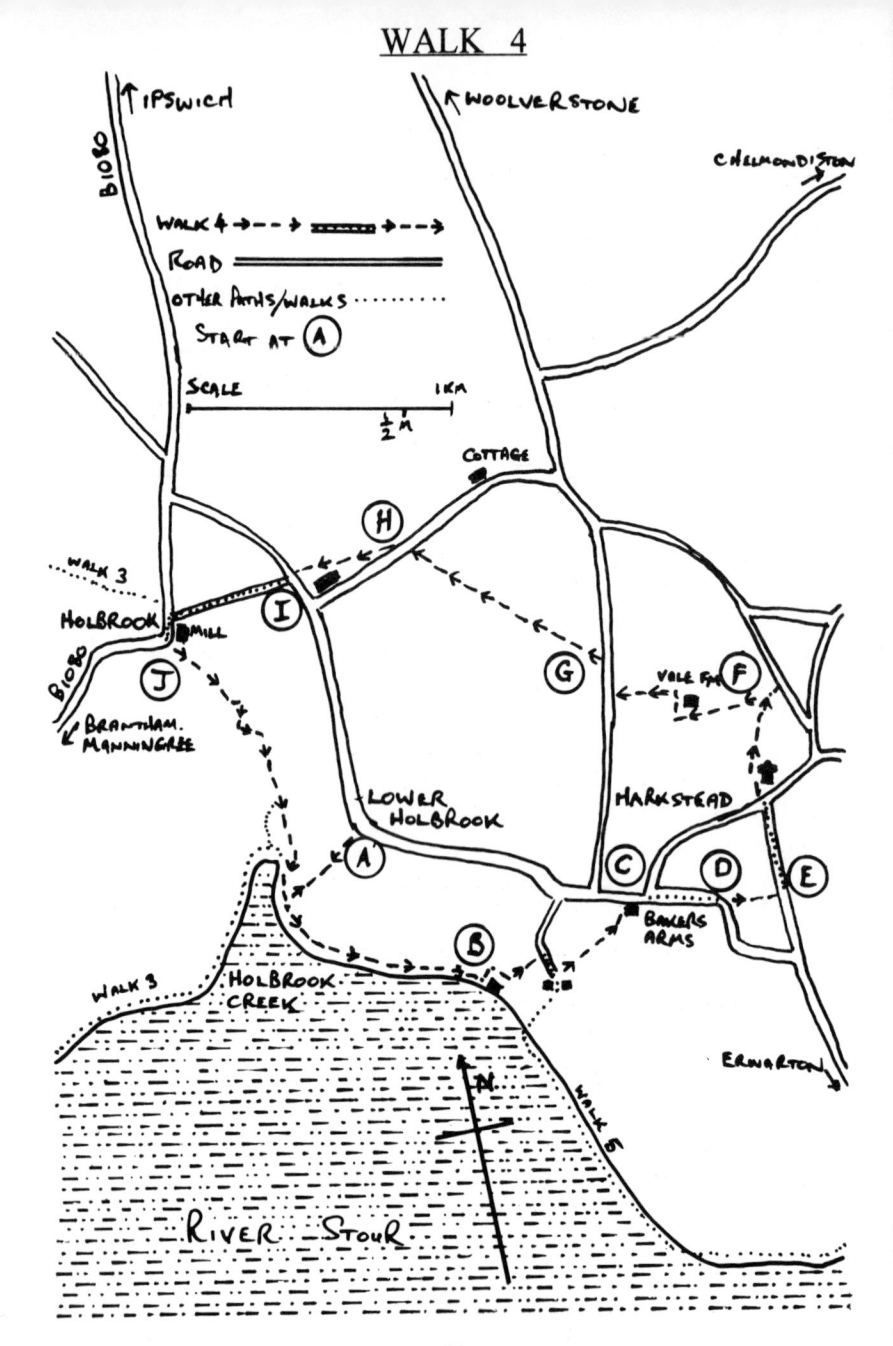

Walk 4

Distance: 8km (5m) 1½-2½ hours
Start Point: Lower Holbrook (GR 177351)
Route: Harkstead, Holbrook Mill, Lower Holbrook
Pub: Baker's Arms, Harkstead
Bus Services: 98
Car Parking: Small free car park in Lower Holbrook

A: Leave the car park and walk down towards the river. Turn left on the river bank for about 1km to reach a cottage.

B: Go round to the left of the cottage and turn left up a track to a narrow road. Turn right on the road for about 200m towards some houses then turn left up a grassy path, bringing you out near the Bakers Arms.

C: Turn right on the road past the Bakers Arms and go straight on for 400m.

D: Where the road bends right, take a path nearly straight on across the field. In 200m cross a footbridge and go up the next field with the hedge on your left.

E: At the road, turn left up towards the church. Cross the stile to the left of the church, and go straight on. After 3 more stiles, keep to the right hand field edge for 50m, then turn left down a wide track towards a farm.

F: Continue on this track, following it round to the left of the farm as far as the driveway. Walk down the driveway to the road, then turn right for about 150m, to find a plank bridge over a ditch on the left.

G: Cross the ditch and walk across the field. (If the path is not clear, stand with your back to the road, and look diagonally right for a red brick cottage by a wood about 600m distant. Now look roughly straight ahead to see another cottage about 1km distant - aim about halfway between these buildings). On the other side of the field, cross a farm track, and continue on the same line. (You may now be able to see a footpath sign on the far side - aim for this if you can).

H: When you reach the road, go straight across and take the footpath on the other side. This leaves the road at a slight angle, and heads straight towards a stile at the left hand end of the field, passing about 50m behind a pair of cottages. Cross the stile and go through a small patch of woodland to the road.

I: Go straight down the road opposite, to reach the main road near Holbrook Mill. Turn left and go past the mill to the bend in the road.

J: Turn left down the unmade road on the bend, keeping to the right on a signed path. The path soon runs parallel to a stream, and you should follow this all the way to the river bank. Turn left when you reach the river for about 150m then left again on the track taking you back to the car park.

WALK 5

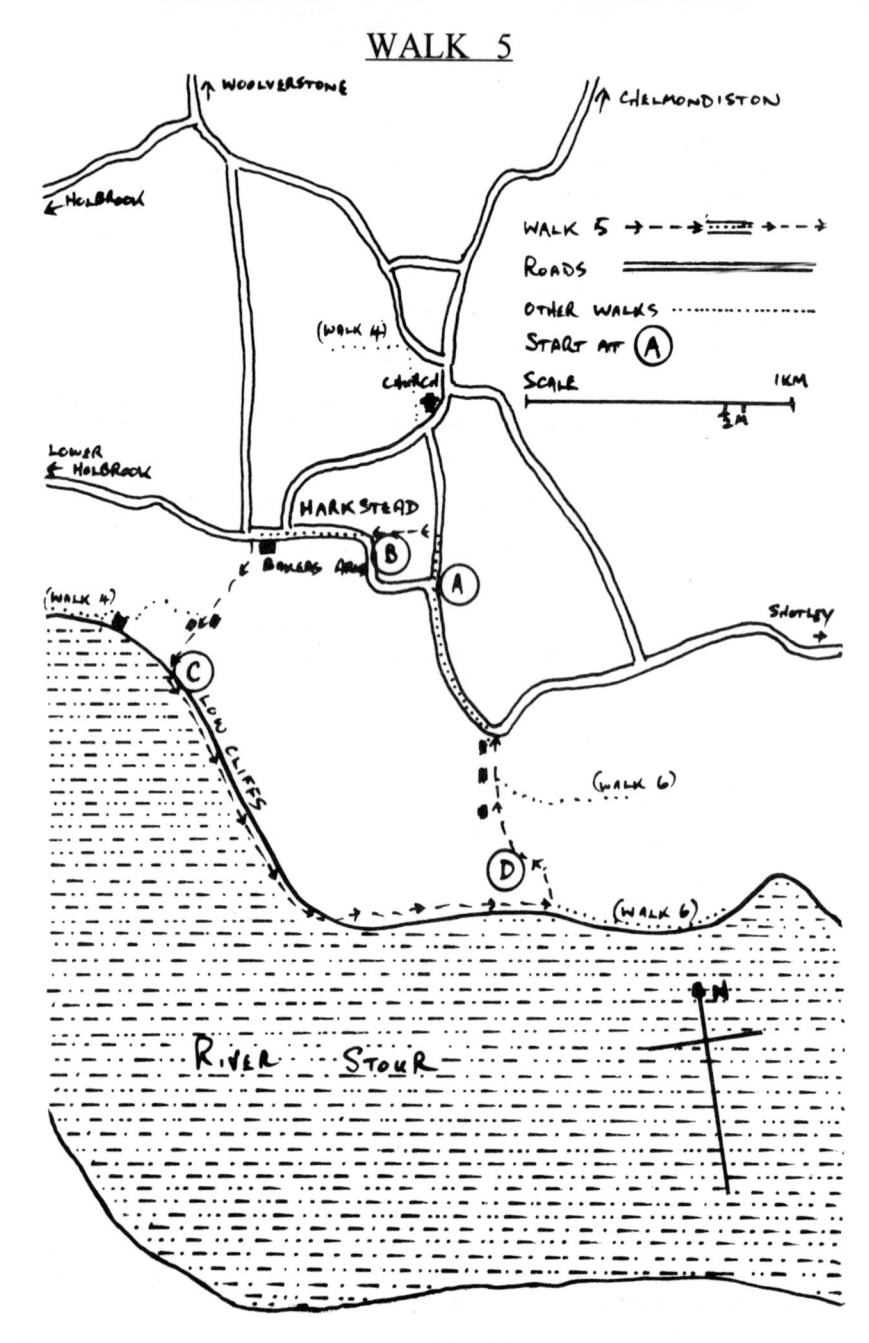

Walk 5

Distance: 5½km (3½m) 1-1½ hours
Start Point: Harkstead (Shotley Road) (GR 195345)
Route: Harkstead circular
Pub: Baker's Arms, Harkstead
Bus Services: 98
Car Parking: Shotley Road, Harkstead

Car parking in Harkstead is difficult, so for this walk I suggest parking on the verge out of the village towards Shotley. To get there, go past the Baker's Arms towards Shotley for about 1km (just over ½ mile) until you see a line of oak trees bordering the road on the left - park on one of the wide verges along here, but beware of drainage gullies.

** At high tides this path may be impassable, since the right of way for the first 1km parallel to the river is along the beach, rather than the field edge. To be on the safe side, don't attempt this path less than 2 hours either side of high tide**.

A: Go back towards Harkstead and take the narrow road up towards the church. In about 200m, turn left on a footpath along the edge of a field. After crossing a bridge over a ditch, go half left up the field on the other side to reach the corner of a road.

B: When you reach the road go straight on to the village. Turn left down the narrow road immediately after the the Bakers Arms then in about 25m go right on a signed path. When you reach a driveway, keep right on a narrow path, and continue down the field. Keep straight on at the houses and follow signs to take you down to the shore.

C: Turn left on the beach - this is the right of way. (If the tide is very high, don't attempt this walk, since the cliffs start to rise along here). After about 1km the cliffs descend to shore level again. About 300m after this, cross a stream on the beach, then cross a narrow strip of marsh to climb to the field edge on your left. Continue along the field edge parallel to the river for a further 800m (about 10 minutes walk).

D: Turn left away from the river on a track along a hedge. In about 100m, at the end of the hedge, bear left on a clear track towards some cottages. Stay on this track, emerging on the Shotley road in about 600m, where you should turn left to return to your car.

WALK 6

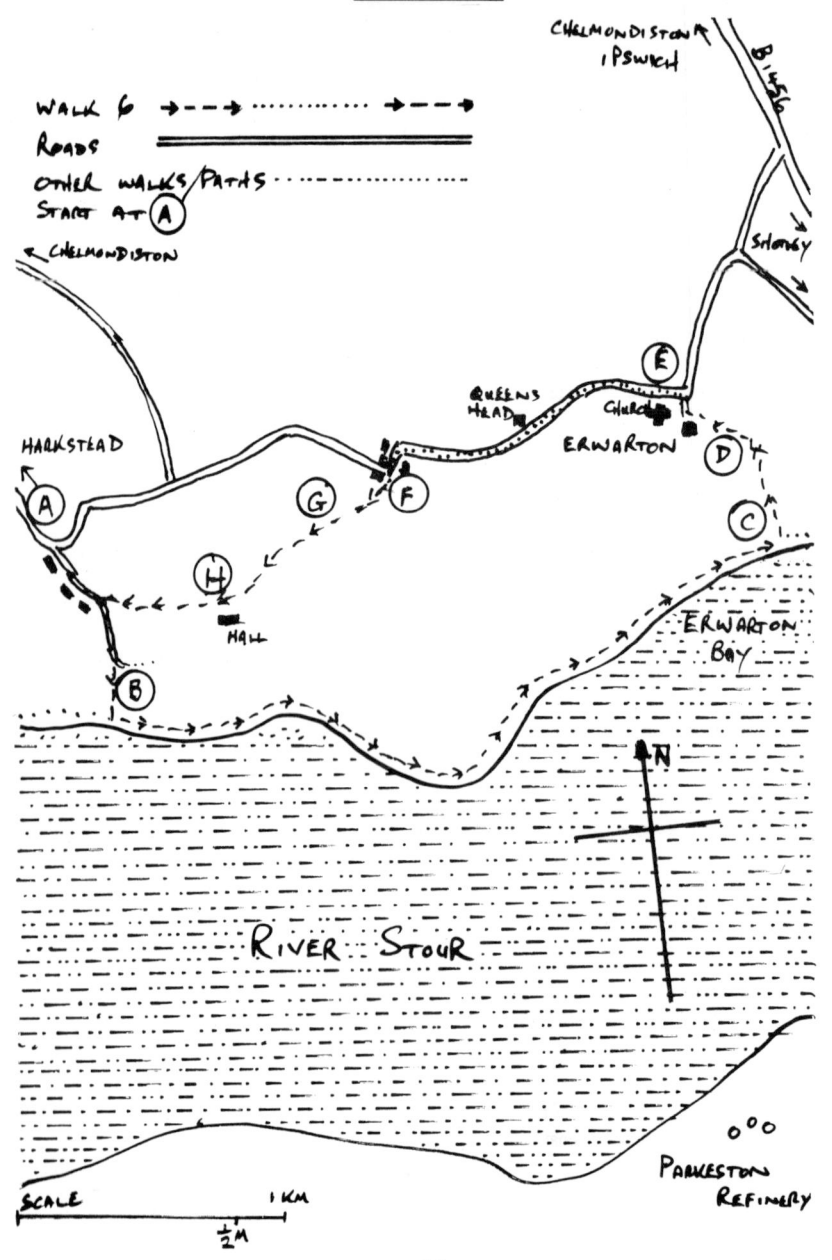

Walk 6

Distance: 8½km (5½m) 2-2½ hours
Start Point: Harkstead-Shotley Road (GR 195345)
Route: Erwarton Shore, Erwarton Church
Pub: Queen's Head, Erwarton
Bus Services: 98
Car Parking: Road side parking between Harkstead and Shotley (See Walk 5)

A: Walk down the road in the Shotley direction, passing a copse on the left. On the next left-hand bend, turn right down a lane next to a pair of brick cottages (signposted 'No Through Road'). Stay on the road, which soon becomes a farm track, and in about 500m take a signed path along a hedge down to the river bank.

B: Turn left on the river bank, following the field edge. Soon the path descends to a river wall, crossing 'Johnny All Alone Creek', then it rises again. After this continue for a further 2km on the field edge path.

C: 300m after passing a small grove of poplars by a reedy pond, turn left on a wide track along a ditch away from the river. In about 400m, just before the last of some trees on the left hand side, cross a plank bridge over the ditch to the left. Continue on the other side of the ditch up to the corner of the field.

D: Turn along the top of the field to a wide gap, go through and continue along the other side of the hedge. In 100m cross a stile and go diagonally across the paddock to a gate in the opposite corner. Go to the top of the lane.

E: Turn left down the road past the church and stay on the road for about 1½km. About 100m after rounding a sharp left hand bend by some houses, go through a gap and go straight on along a field edge where the road bends sharp right.

F: Go along the edge of the field with the hedge on your right. After about 200m you'll come to a large field. If the route is not clear, aim about 100m to the right of the farm buildings across the fields in front of you. At the bottom of the field you'll find a stile to take you into the right-hand corner of a rough meadow.

G: Aim slightly left to cross another stile on the other side of the meadow, crossing a stream via a plank bridge on the way. *The definitive right of way in the next field is diagonally across from the stile to the road next to the farm buildings. However, the width of the headland suggests the preferred route is the field edge.* If the path is apparent across the field, use it, otherwise follow the field edge.

H: On the other side of the road, go between two redundant gateposts and cross the field towards the leftmost of 3 buildings. When you reach the next field edge, change course slightly to follow the left hand edge of a ditch towards the middle building. Turn right when you reach the lane and walk back to your start point.

WALK 7

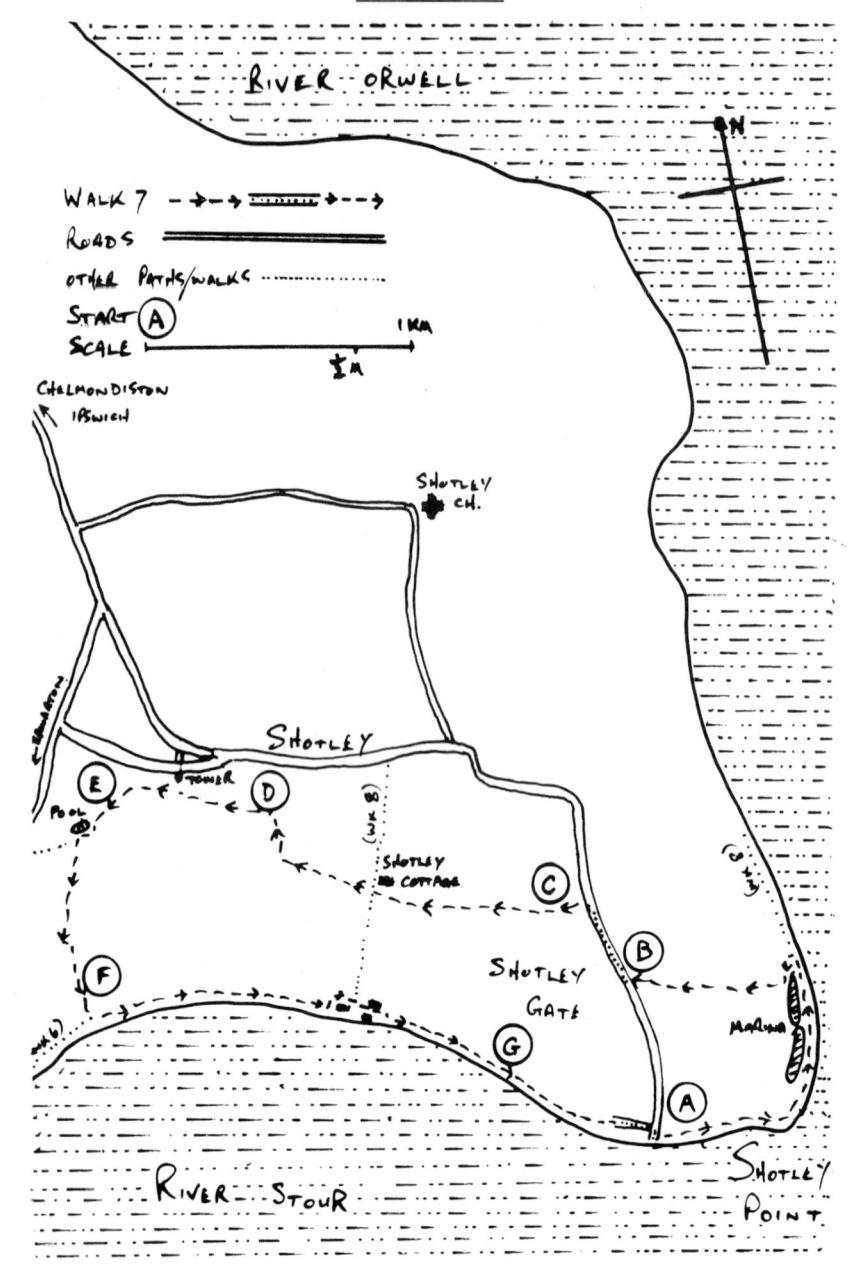

Walk 7

Distance: 8km (5m) 1½-2 hours
Start Point: Shotley Gate (GR 246336)
Route: Shotley Point, Marina, Erwarton, Foreshore
Pub: Bristol Arms
Bus Services: 97, 97A, 98
Car Parking: Car Parking opposite Bristol Arms

A: Walk along the quayside with the river on your right. Keep to the river side of the Marina, cross the lockgate and continue along the wide bank on the other side. *This right of way is under review at the time of writing - please observe any signs indicating future changes of route* At the end of the marina, go back along the road for about 50m, then go through a gap into the field, and turn up the field edge to the top. Turn right at the top and walk along the field edge into a grassy lane, and onward to the road.

B: Turn right on the road and in about 300m, when you reach the end of the row of houses on the left, take a clear signed track to the left.

C: Follow this track for about 1km to Shotley cottage, then continue in the same direction on a grassy footpath. In about 400m you'll come to a large field. *The right of way here is almost straight on, but a better alternative is in use further up the field*. Turn right along the field edge for about 150m, until you are level with the back gardens of some houses.

D: At this point turn left across the field. Cross the narrow lane level with the water tower, then bear very slightly right towards a stile by a small clump of trees.

E: Cross the stile, and go half-left down to another stile. Follow the path round to the left of a pool, and when you get to the other side, just before reaching another stile, turn left on a grassy track towards the river. Stay on this to the river bank.

F: Turn left on the river bank. In about 1km you'll reach a cluster of cottages. Follow signs here to take you through to the river bank path on the other side. In 500m you'll enter some trees, then emerge onto a road.

G: Stay on the verge on the right-hand side, and in about 50m take the signed path into the trees. Continue on this meandering shady path for about 500m, finally emerging onto a road on a corner. Turn right on a signed path along a fence parallel to the river, soon taking you to a made road. Follow this down to the bottom and turn right, bringing you back to the car park.

WALK 8

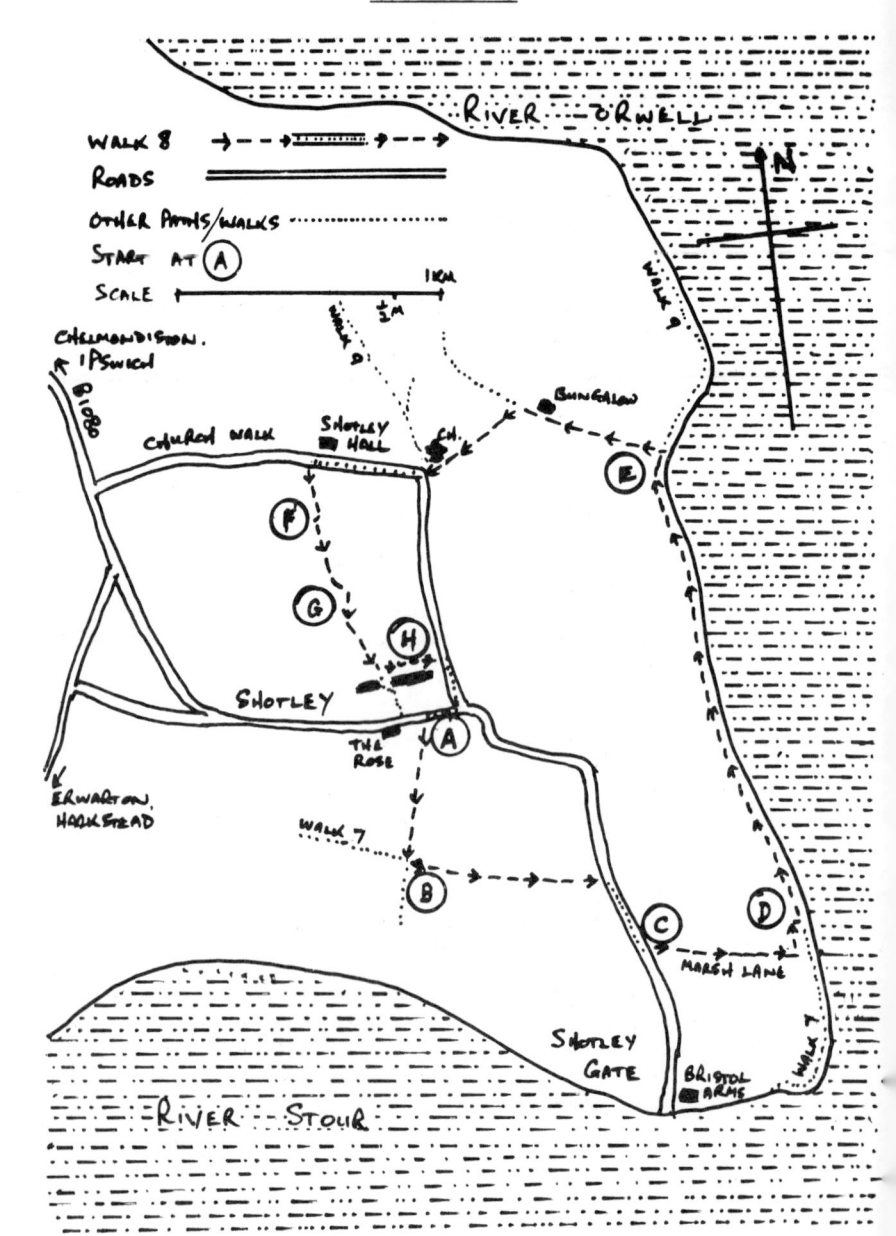

Walk 8

Distance: 8km (5m) 1½-2 hours
Start Point: Main Road, Shotley (GR 237352)
Route: Shotley Gate, Marina, Foreshore, Shotley Church
Pub: The Rose
Bus Services: 97, 97A, 98
Car Parking: Lay by 300m on the Shotley Gate side of The Rose pub.

A: Walk back towards The Rose, and in 200m go left on a signed path through Rose Farm. Continue down for 500m to Shotley Cottage, then turn left.

B: Follow this track for about 1km until you reach a road. Turn right on the road and after about 300m turn left down a grassy lane next to playing fields.

C: Follow the lane, eventually becoming a field-edge path, almost down to the river. When you get to the end, turn left down the field edge for about 50m then go through a gap to reach the river wall.

D: Turn left along the river wall and follow it for about 2km. **The square stone along here isn't a memorial to 2 departed walkers, but a boundary stone between Harwich Harbour Board, and Ipswich Port Authority!***

E: Just before the river wall merges with a rising field edge lined by bushes, turn left, cross a stile and go along the edge of the field towards Shotley Church. Pass a bungalow, then turn left along the 'R.U.P.P.' (road used as public path) up the hill, past the quaintly but aptly named 'No 1. Below the Church'.

Continue on past the church, and in about 500m, shortly after passing the attractive Shotley Hall, turn left down a signposted lane.

F: About 100m after the end of the trees on the left-hand side of the lane, go down through a gap on the right to continue downhill on the other side of the hedge. (N. B. The second gap on the right-hand side).

G: Soon the field edge bends to the left, and, shortly after this, turn right across the field to a footbridge. Cross the bridge, then follow the path up the field. **The definitive right of way is along the left hand side of the hedge for some distance, but local usage is along the right hand side all the way to the top**

H: Take the path to the left along the back of the houses at the top of the hill, emerging on a narrow road in about 500m. Turn right on the road and right again at the top to return to the start-point.

WALK 9

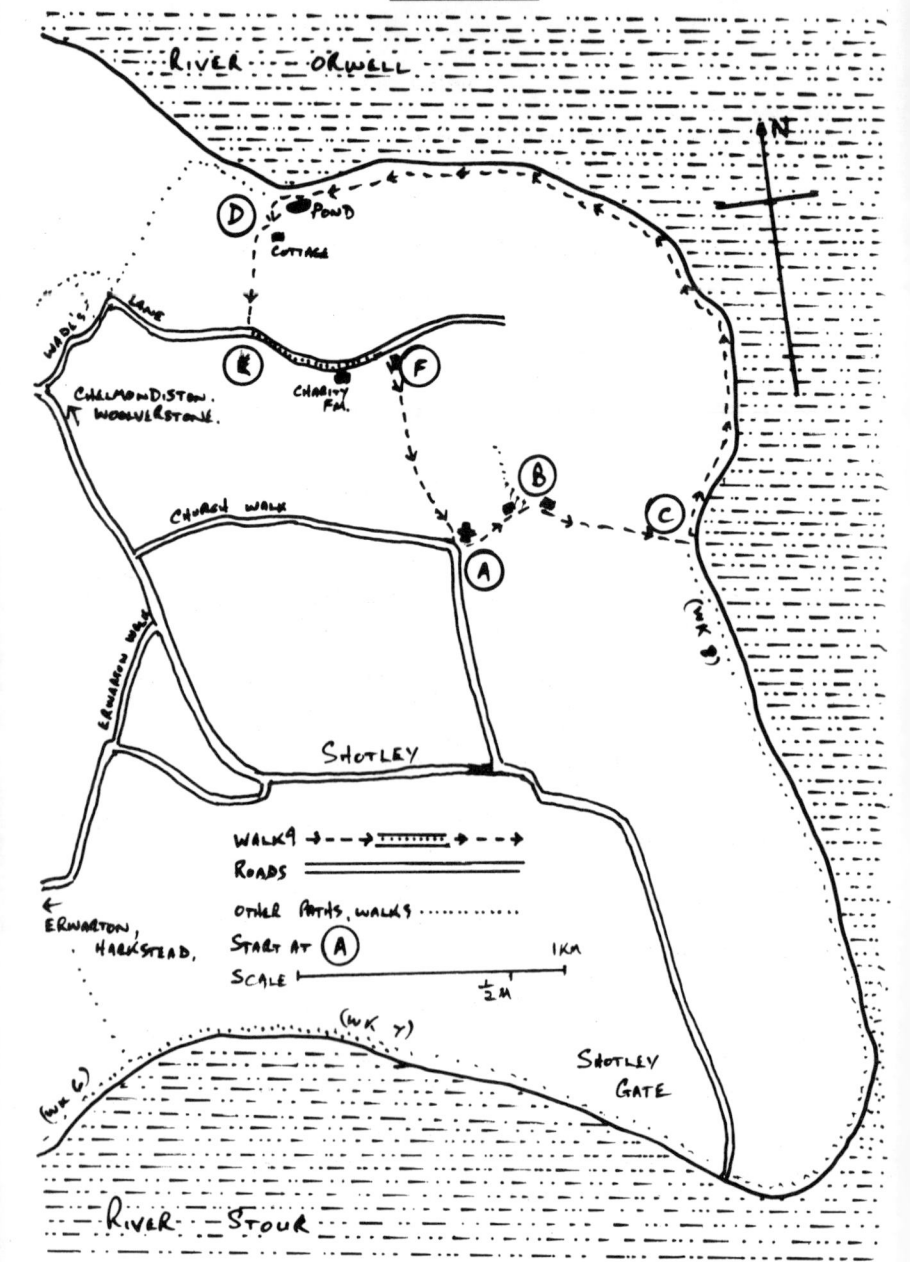

Walk 9

Distance: 6½km (4m) 1½ hours app.
Start Point: Shotley Church (GR 237360)
Route: River wall, Wade's Lane
Pub: No
Bus Services: 97, 97A, 98 (Main road Shotley only)
Car Parking: Large car park behind Shotley Church - please give priority to church users. (A 50p donation to the church is suggested for use of the car park).

A: Go round to the front of the church, and go down the track between the church and the naval cemetery.

B: At the T-junction at the bottom of the hill, turn right, cross the stile just past the bungalow, then follow the field-edge along to the river wall.

C: Climb onto the river wall, turn left, then descend onto the marsh for about 150m to reach the river wall again. Stay on the wall now for about 2½km passing Levington Marina on the other side of the river.

D: Eventually the river wall path merges with a well surfaced track by a small patch of woodland. The track skirts a pond, and shortly afterwards a cottage. Follow the track away from the river up to the road. (Wade's Lane)

E: Turn left in Wade's Lane and continue along for about 600m. About 100m after passing Charity Farm turn right on a signposted track by a bungalow. (Upper Lodge)

F: Follow this track for about 800m back to the church.

WALK 10

Walk 10

Distance: 4km (2½m) 1 hour approx
Start Point: Pin Mill (GR206378)
Route: Clamp House, N.T. Woods
Pub: Butt and Oyster
Bus Services: 97, 97A, 98 (Chelmondiston only)
Car Parking: Public Car Park in Pin Mill

A: Go through the picnic site next to the Pin Mill car park, and cross the stile at the far end. Turn right into the field and walk diagonally up to the top right hand corner. Cross the stile and continue up the lane.

B: At the top, turn left towards the church. Bear left round the church on a narrow road and continue to a T-junction. Go straight across onto a signed footpath.

C: In about 100m the path joins a farm road. Follow the road, which soon becomes a cart track, for about 1½km. Eventually you'll come to a gate accessing a lane to Clamp House. Cross the stile to enter the lane and continue down towards the river.

D: Just after passing a reedy pond on the left, turn left into the National Trust woods. Stay on the main path, parallel to the river, for about 700m, until you reach the bottom of a steep hill. Here, if the tide is low enough, you have the option of turning right and following the permissive path along the bank to reach the Butt and Oyster. However, if the tide is high, you won't be able to get along the shore by the pub, so stay on the main path to reach the road near the car park.

WALK 11

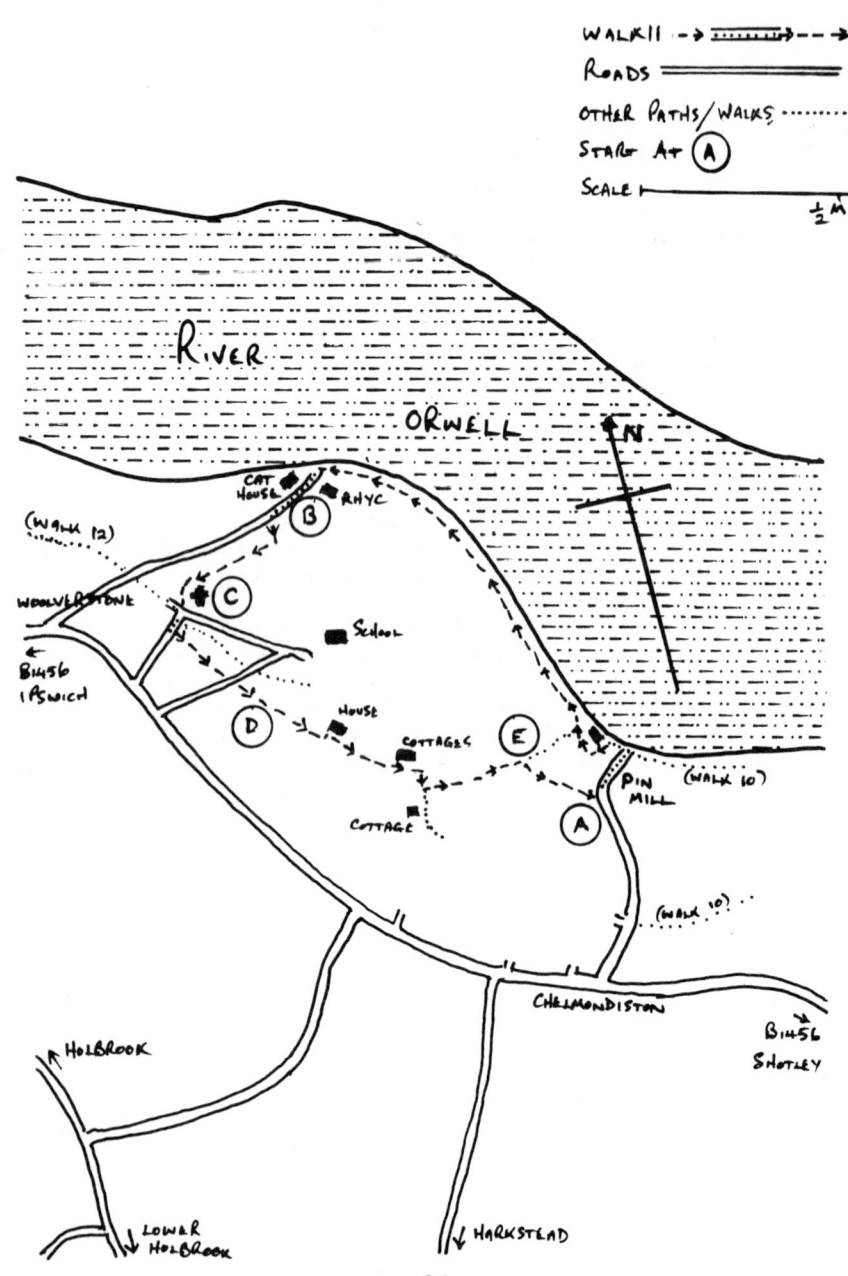

Walk 11

Distance: 4½km (3m) 1-1½ hours.
Start Point: Pin Mill (GR 206378)
Route: Woolverstone Marina, Cat House, Pin Mill
Pub: Butt and Oyster.
Bus Services: 97, 97A, 98 (Chelmondiston only)
Car Parking: Public car park in Pin Mill

A: Go down the road towards the river and turn left along the unmade road at the bottom. In about 100m follow the track round by the clubhouse, then in a further 50m turn right along a shady lane.

The lane soon enters open fields. Continue more or less parallel to the river for about 1½km to reach Woolverstone Marina. Follow the signs keeping you to the river side of the Royal Harwich Yacht Club, then turn left up a metalled road next to the Cat House.

B: Continue up the road for about 300m then take a signed footpath down some steps into a pleasant valley on the left. Follow the path up the valley to bring you out behind Woolverstone church.

C: Go round to the front of the church. On the left-hand side of the road opposite there are 2 footpath signs a short distance apart. Take the second of these paths. After crossing 4 stiles you'll reach a field edge path.

D: Go along the field edge to a large new house, then continue on the same line along a part-metalled lane. After passing a pair of cottages, the lane bends to the right. Shortly afterwards turn left on a clear signed track. Where the track bends to the left across the field, keep along the field edge.

E: When you reach the end of the woodland on the right hand side, take a signed Countryside Commission permissive path down through the field on the right. Keeping to the fence on the right, go through a gap at the bottom, and continue downhill to a stile. Cross the stream, bear slightly left to avoid a marshy area, then head uphill to the top left hand corner to a gate and a stile at the top of the field. Cross this and go straight ahead to reach the picnic site next to the car park.

WALK 12

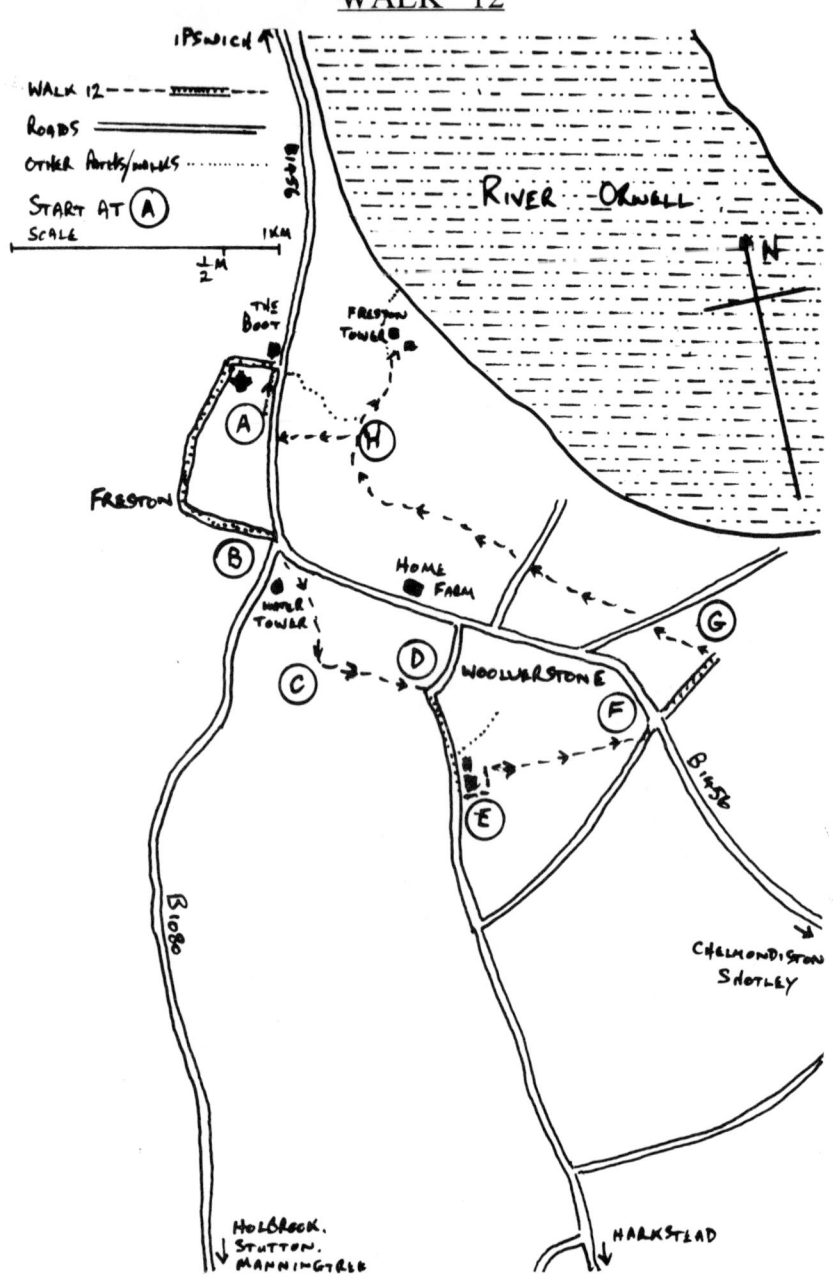

Walk 12

Distance: 7½km (4½m) 1½ - 2 hours
Start Point: Freston (GR 174395)
Route: Freston Church, Woolverstone Church, Freston Tower
Pub: The Boot
Bus Services: 96, 97, 97A, 98, 639
Car Parking: Lay-by 300m past The Boot approaching from Ipswich

A: Go back to the Boot and turn left down the narrow road signposted Freston. Follow the road round past the church to the village. Turn left at the T-junction.

B: At the corner near the water tower, cross the road and take the footpath through the gap to cross the field to the left of the tower.

C: After crossing two fields, turn left on a signed path, soon walking on a field edge path along a hawthorn hedge, more or less parallel to the road in Woolverstone. After a brief 'left and right' continue straight on until you reach a narrow road.

D: Turn right on the road, and stay on it for about 400m, passing two buildings on the left. After passing the garden of the second cottage turn left at a footpath sign.

E: Almost immediately, turn left through a wire mesh fence to pass between the garden and a thicket. When you reach the field, go half-right towards a gap in the hedge on the far side. Go through the gap to enter the next field at a corner. Continue on more or less the same diagonal line to a gap in the opposite corner, to emerge on a narrow road.

F: Turn left on the road, and in about 100m go straight across past the lodge to the access road to Woolverstone Church. Continue down here to the T-junction by the church, where you should turn left.

G: Follow this pleasant track for about 1½km crossing two metalled roads on the way. After crossing the 2nd metalled road, the track becomes a field edge path. Then, after passing Home Farm over the field to your left, the path becomes a metalled lane and starts to swing right. Soon there's another swing to the right, and you'll be heading directly towards Freston Tower.

H: If you don't want to see the Tower, watch out for a signed footpath along an unmade road to the left. This will take you back to the lay-by.

To see the tower, continue down the lane. From the cattle grid, cut across the grass towards the left fence of the house to reach the tower.

After seeing the tower, retrace your steps to the unmade road leading to the lay-by. (The signed path along the edge of the wood will bring you out opposite the Boot).

WALK 13

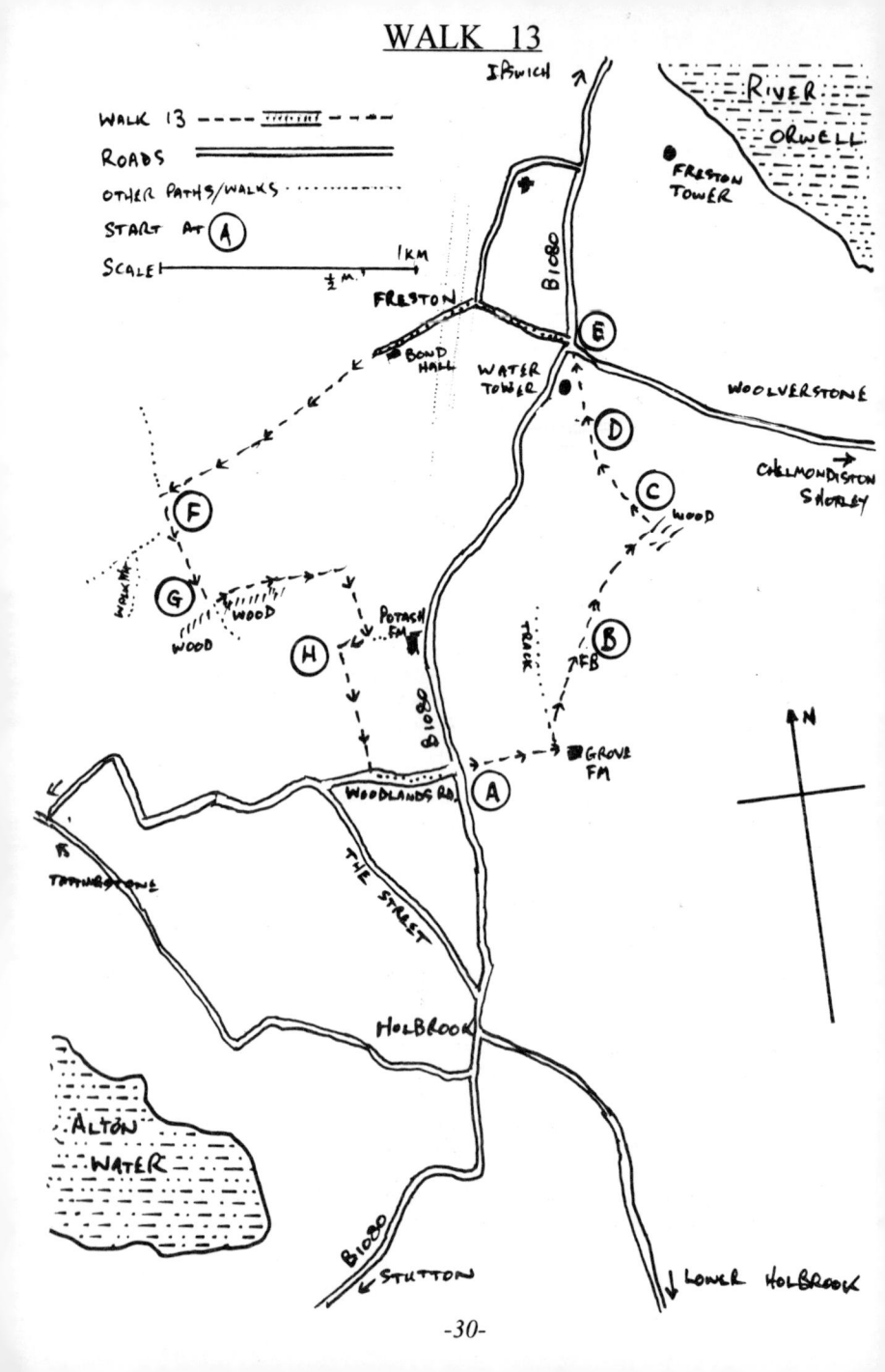

Walk 13

Distance: 8m (5m) 1½ - 2 hours
Start Point: Holbrook (GR 169373)
Route: Freston, Holbrook
Bus Services: 96, 97A, 98, 639
Car Parking: Small Lay-by opposite Woodlands Road on B1080 at the Ipswich end of Holbrook.

A: Go down the lane opposite Woodlands Road. Just before farm buildings, turn left on a farm track. In about 50m take a path half right across the field. (If the path is not clear, aim towards 2 trees on a field edge in the valley).

B: Cross the footbridge by the trees, and continue on more or less the same line up the field on the other side. (If the path isn't clear, follow the direction of the yellow arrow - when you get a bit higher in the field you'll be able to see a small wood in front of you - aim for the left hand edge).

C: A few metres after passing through a gap in the field edge to the left of the wood, turn left on a signed path, almost directly towards the water tower. This should bring you to a footpath sign at the right hand end of a hawthorn hedge.

D: Go more or less straight on across the next field, heading towards the power line support to the right of the water tower. At the next field edge continue on the same line to emerge on the road at a four-way junction.

E: Cross the road on your left and go down the road signed 'Freston'. Pass through the village, and continue past Bond Hall on a private road. ***This private road is not a right of way, although the owners allow people to use it - However, they do reserve the right to refuse passage if such use is abused** Go straight on past a farm onto a bridleway on an unmade farm track. In about 1km after passing some woodland on the right you'll reach a T-junction of paths.

F: Turn left at the T-junction, and go straight on for about 350m to a strip of woodland. **The path to your right about 50m along here links with Walk 14***

G: Don't go through the woodland, but turn left down a track along the edge. Continue on the track after the end of the wood across the open field. Follow the track round to the right in about 300m.

H: Where the track bends left to a farm (Potash Farm), turn right. In 100m turn left along a path between two unhedged fields, aiming directly towards the left hand side of a tall hedge bordering a garden on the other side of the field.

I: At the road turn left and walk along to your car on the main road.

WALK 14

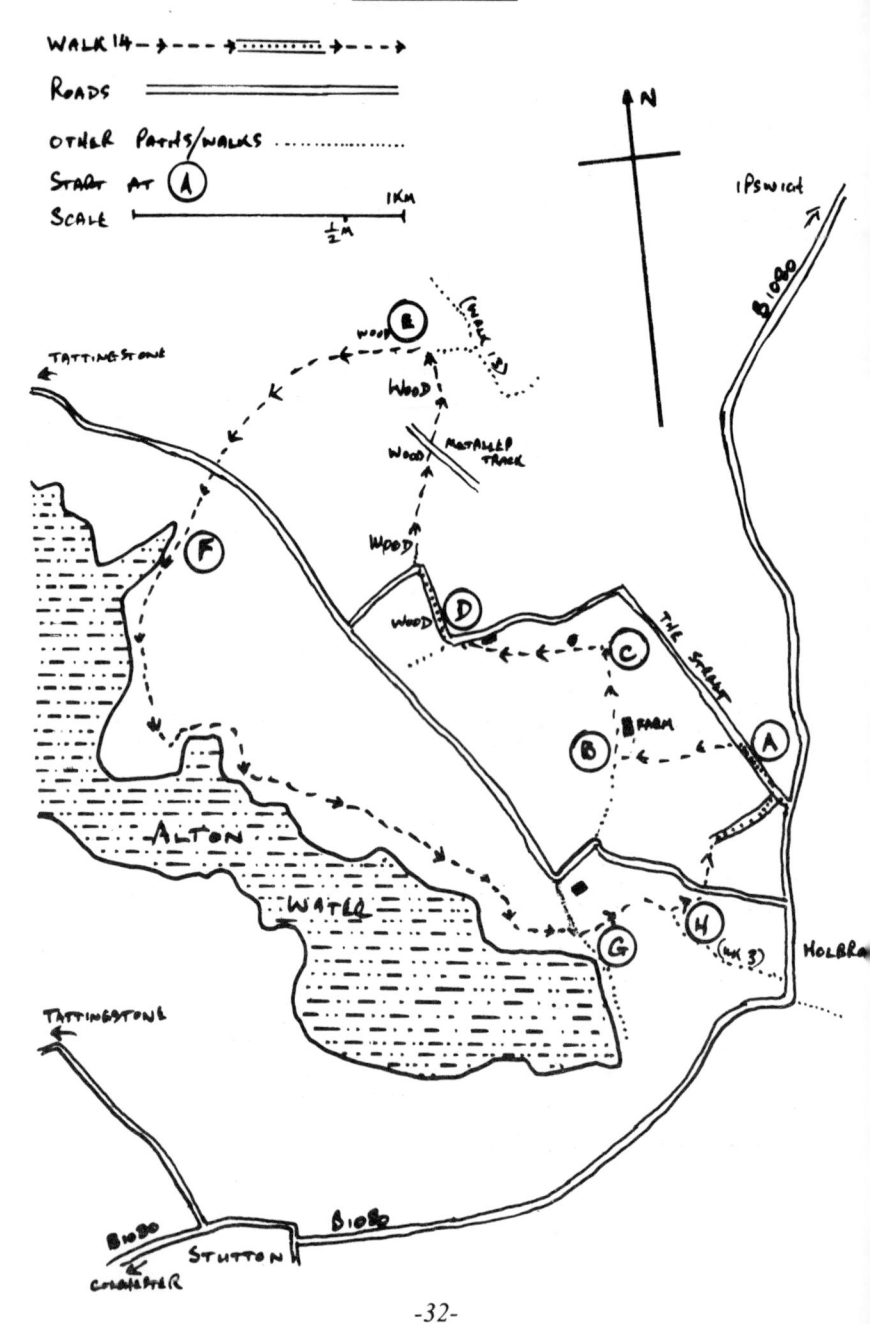

Walk 14

Distance: 9½km (6m) 2 - 2½ hour
Start Point: Holbrook Village Hall (The Street) (GR 167366)
Route: Alton Water, Holbrook
Pub: The Swan
Bus Services: 96, 97A, 98, 639
Car Parking: In 'The Street', past the Village Hall, where the road widens

A: Go down a track almost opposite the Village Hall. After passing through a metal kissing gate, and alongside a playing field, cross the road and continue on the track on the other side. Where the track turns sharp right at the bottom of the hill, continue staight on up the field.

B: Turn right on the other side of the field edge and walk past the farmhouse to a farm track. Go down the left hand side of the corrugated iron building on the signed path. Go straight on when you reach the end of the buildings. Watch for a tree and a small sign on an incomplete field edge on your left.

C: When you're abreast of the tree turn left towards it on a cross path, and continue on the same line towards woods about 600m distant, aiming to the left of a house in a clump of trees. This brings you out on the corner of a road.

D: Follow the road round to the right. When the road bends left in about 300m, continue along the edge of the wood on a signed path. In about 150m bear slightly right to a power line support on the corner of another wood. Follow the edge round, crossing a metalled track in about 50m. After the metalled track, continue along the edge of the wood for a further 350m.

E: Turn left on a bridleway into the wood through a gateway, (where a track crosses the field from the right). Continue through the wood, keeping right where the track forks in about 200m, to reach a field edge track on the far side. Go along the track to a road and take a signed footpath down to Alton Water.

F: Turn to the left round Alton Water. Generally speaking the best route to take is the higher cycle track, remaining within the perimeter fence. This is the shortest route, and gives the better views.

G: Just before passing through the wide farm-type wooden gate onto the concrete 'built-up' area of the reservoir, take a footpath to the left downhill alongside a high wire fence, then some trees. (Not the signed path down towards the cottages).

H: About 100m after crossing a footbridge at the bottom of the hill, take a footpath to the left to bring you up to a road in about 100m. Go straight across the road, and along an unmade road by some terraced houses. In a further 200m turn right onto a road, and continue along here to the T-junction, where you should turn left to bring you back to the village hall.

WALK 15

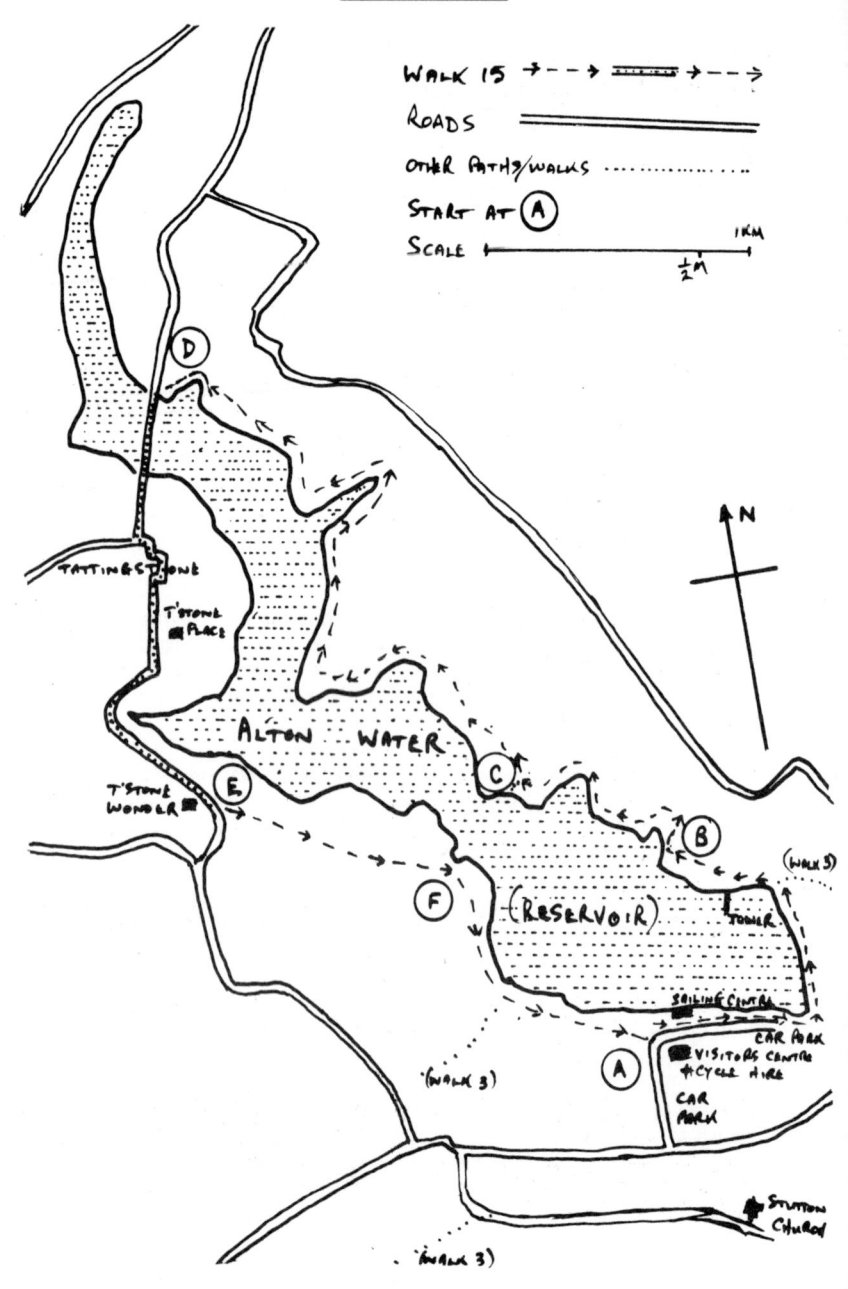

Walk 15

Distance: 12m (8m) 2½ - 3½ hours
Start Point: Alton Water Visitors Centre (GR 156354)
Route: Alton Water circular via Tattingstone Wonder,
Pub: The Orange Box (Tattingstone)
Bus Services: 96, 97A, 639
Car Parking: Pay and Display car park near Visitors Centre

A: Go down to the perimeter road and turn right. Walk round the reservoir in an anti-clockwise direction.

Walking round the reservoir in an anti-clockwise direction is a good idea because, when you reach the the only place of refreshment, in Tattingstone, you'll already have completed two thirds of your walk - far better than still having most of it to do!

When faced with a choice of paths, favour the higher one, remaining within the perimeter fence. For the most part, the best route is signed, either as a footpath or cycle route, and tends to keep to the higher ground, giving better views and a shorter walk

B: Stay on the main path, observing footpath/cycleway signs where necessary.

C: The path downhill to the left of Crag Hall wood may look tempting but keep along the right hand edge to the top and then turn left. Continue on the main path for about another 4km, to reach Lemons Hill Bridge.

D: Cross the bridge, and go up the road into Tattingstone. Turn left at the T-junction, passing the Orange Box pub cum post office on your left. Stay on the recommended cycle route, which takes you along the road for about 2km as far as the Tattingstone Wonder (this looks like a church, but is actually a row of cottages).

E: Here turn left on the cycle path, and stay on this all the way back to the Visitors Centre.

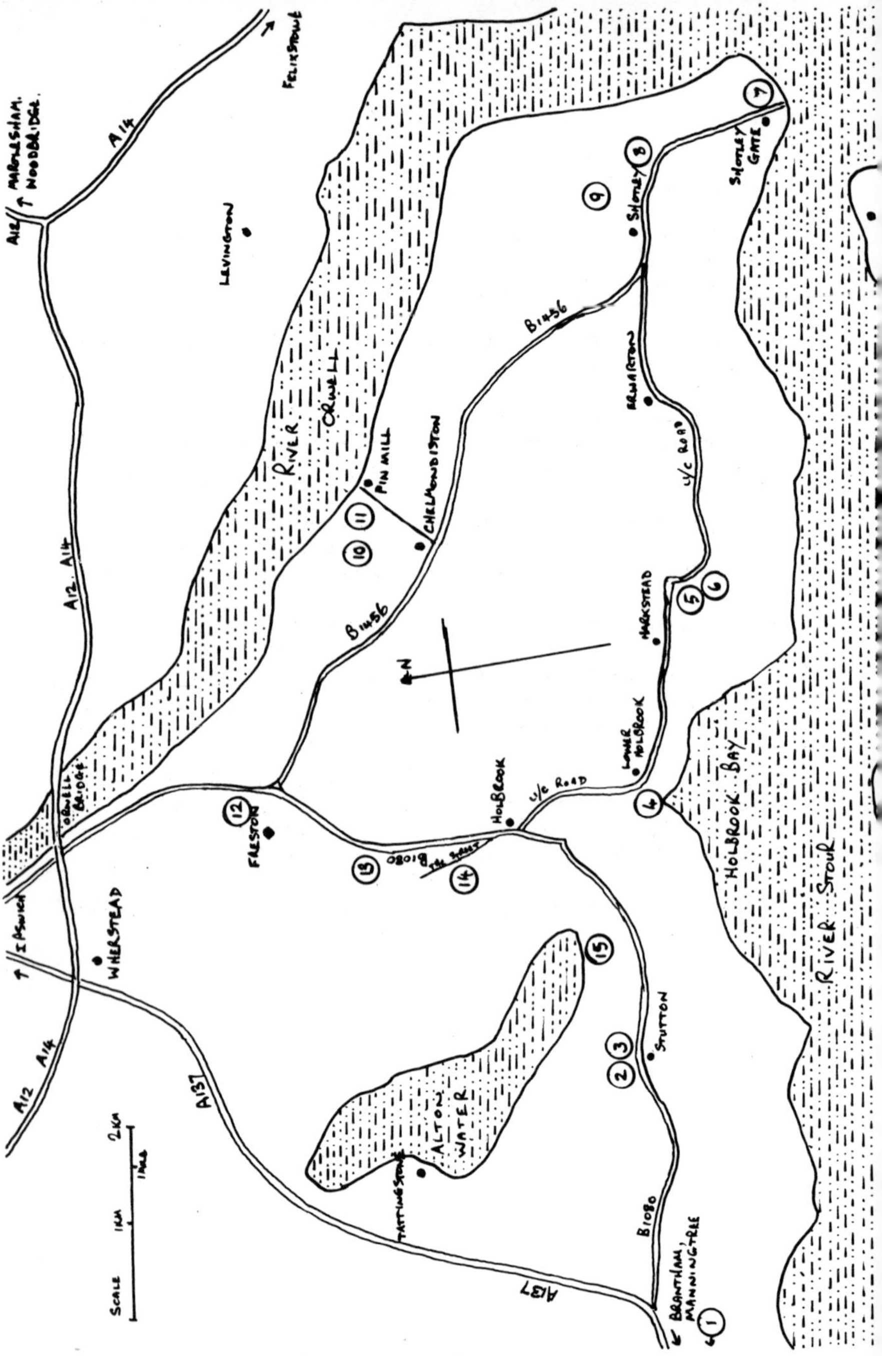
IPSWICH
WHERSTEAD
A12 A14
A12 A14
A12
A14
MARTLESHAM, WOODBRIDGE
FELIXSTOWE
LEVINGTON
ORWELL BRIDGE
RIVER ORWELL
PIN MILL
CHELMONDISTON
B1456
B1456
FRESTON
B1080
HOLBROOK
U/C ROAD
LOWER HOLBROOK
HARKSTEAD
ERWARTON
U/C ROAD
SHOTLEY
SHOTLEY GATE
HOLBROOK BAY
RIVER STOUR
ALTON WATER
TATTINGSTONE
STUTTON
B1080
A137
A137
BRANTHAM, MANNINGTREE
SCALE
1KM
2KM
1MILE
N
1
2
3
4
5
6
7
8
9
10
11
12
13
14
15